Golden Bubbles

A Grandmother's Journey through Grief

Edna Butterfield, Ed.D.

Publishing Designs, Inc.
Huntsville, Alabama

Publishing Designs, Inc.
P.O. Box 3241
Huntsville, Alabama 35810

Printed in the United States of America

Library of Congress Cataloging-in-Publication Data

Butterfield, Edna, 1941-

Golden bubbles : learning through loss : a grandmother's insight into childhood cancer / Edna Butterfield.

    p. cm.

ISBN 978-0-929540-64-1 (alk. paper)

1. Children—Death—Religious aspects—Christianity. 2. Loss (Psychology)—Religious aspects—Christianity. 3. Consolation. 4. Suffering—Religious aspects—Christianity. 5. Bereavement—Religious aspects—Christianity. 6. Grief—Religious aspects—Christianity. 7. Cancer in children—Religious aspects—Christianity. 8. Lymphomas—Patients. I. Title.

BV4907.B88 2007

  248.8'66—dc22

2007000034

Dedication

To my grandchildren

Contents

Introduction

When my two-year-old granddaughter, Alyson, was diagnosed with lymphoma, I saw many grandparents at the hospital who, although distraught, were willingly helping with the care of their grandchildren with similar diagnoses. As Alyson's two-year-plus treatment began, I decided to write a book to help grandparents cope with this painful time of fears and distress. The title was to be *Bubbles and Ballerinas: A Grandparent's Look at Childhood Cancer*. It was to be a positive book of hope, a book about how grandparents can do more than cope with their grandchild's cancer. I knew that grandparents could relieve some of the burden from their children through knowing what to do to be helpful.

The title came from some of the conversations I had with Alyson about growing up. She had begun talking very early. By the time she was two, her conversations were very adult-like. Alyson told me the two things she wanted to do when she grew up: be a ballerina and blow bubbles. I had inwardly laughed about the ballerina wish. Alyson was built more like a little tank than a willowy ballerina. I questioned her concerning blowing bubbles. I knew she had been blowing soap bubbles before she was a year old. She said, "Nana, I don't want to blow soap bubbles. I want to blow gum bubbles like Meghan does." To Alyson, Meghan, her six-year-old sister, was "grown up."

Then the unthinkable happened. A year after the diagnosis, Alyson lost her battle with cancer and I abandoned the idea of a book. She would never be six; she would never even be four. She would never blow gum bubbles. Who wanted to read a book about a child who died of cancer? I didn't want to write about a lost battle. During the difficult year of Alyson's treatment, my daughter, Leanne (Alyson's mother) and I had read many books about children with cancer. We always read the last chapter first. If the child died, the book remained unread. We needed hope and encouragement at that time, not a devastatingly sad ending.

My idea of a book for grandparents about dealing with cancer now seemed unthinkable. My heart was not in helping anyone who was going through cancer. What could I say to them? Cancer had claimed the life of our precious Alyson. It seemed an ugly thing—a thing to forget. The idea of writing any book was cast aside.

Then my daughter asked a question—a question that inspired this book: *Mom, what do you think God was trying to teach us through this?* I decided to write a book about coping with loss, a subject with which I was wrestling.

I also changed the title due to a conversation with Alyson's now seven-year-old sister, Meghan, about the wish to grow up to "blow gum bubbles." I asked Meghan, "Do you think Alyson will get to blow bubbles in heaven?" "Yes, Nana," she said. "Golden bubbles!"

Because I have changed from a grandmother dealing with a grandchild's cancer to a grandmother in the process of healing from a tragic loss, the book title *Golden Bubbles* has evolved with this description: "A Grandmother's Journey through Grief." Although I wrote this book for my own healing, I pray that it may also help those of you who are struggling with loss.

When I am afraid,
I will put my trust in You

Psalm 56:3

Alyson's wish fulfilled by seeing
Cinderella at Disneyworld

Chapter 1

Alyson's Story

A Normal Day

November 10, 1999, was a bright, crisp day in west Tennessee. Long sighs of relief could be heard in every office of the School of Education at Freed-Hardeman University, a Christian college in the small town of Henderson. The National Council for the Accreditation of Teacher Education (NCATE) team would be leaving campus today. Everything appeared to have gone well. In a few minutes my husband, Ron, the dean of the School of Education, would participate in an exit interview with the team. My bags were packed. Two other Freed-Hardeman teachers and I were ready to head to New Orleans for an early childhood teachers' conference.

9

Ron was planning to stay home and, as he said, "do as little as possible." We all needed a break from the past few months of intense preparation for the NCATE visit.

Three World-Shattering Words

As I was heading down the hall from my office, the secretary said I had a phone call from my son-in-law, Bryan. I knew something was wrong when I heard his voice. After a brief hello, he said, "Alyson has lymphoma." I know I heard the rest of the conversation, but nothing else registered. My world was shattered by those three words. After I hung up the phone I rushed down the hall and fell crying into my colleague Pat's arms. Trying to be comforting, she said, "Maybe it's not a correct diagnosis." But I knew it was accurate; the diagnosis had been the result of an examination of lymph node tissue sent to Mayo Clinic following a tonsillectomy a few days before. Alyson's pediatrician, having had some concerns about a swollen lymph node, had decided to have it surgically removed and checked as a precautionary measure. We truly thought it was simply that—precautionary.

Her light brown curls would bounce as she giggled and said, "Do it again." If any two-and-a-half-year-old looked the picture of health, it was Alyson.

I couldn't let Ron see me crying. He couldn't know about Alyson until after the exit interview. He had to be alert for the next hour. Quickly and mechanically, I drove home. A few minutes later a good friend, my walking partner, Debbie, arrived to comfort me. Ron's administrative assistant, Rhonda, had called her. I felt immobilized by the news. My son, Brian, who also teaches at Freed-Hardeman, came. He was as devastated as I. He and Alyson had bonded from the time she was a tiny baby. She liked to have Uncle Brian set her upside down and then turn her chubby little body over into a somersault. Her light brown curls would bounce as she giggled and said, "Do it again." If any two-and-a-half-year-old looked the picture of health, it was Alyson.

Changes and Tests

As soon as the exit interview was over, Jim, the Director of the Graduate Program, told Ron the terrible news. In a matter of minutes Ron was home holding me as I sobbed. I was all packed for a business trip, but those New Orleans plans had changed radically. Ron packed quickly. We were on our way to Atlanta where our daughter Leanne, her husband Bryan, and their two children, six-year-old Meghan and little Alyson lived. I prayed silently most of the way. Ron and I talked very little. I knew I couldn't fall apart when I got there. I was almost sure our daughter would not be crying. She would be keeping things together for the children and Bryan. I had always been amazed at her strength. And now that strength was to be tested.

The pediatrician sent Alyson to the hospital for preliminary tests on the tenth—the day we got the call—but she would not be admitted nor would her chemo start until the eleventh. I accompanied Bryan, Leanne, and Alyson to the hospital. The tests had revealed a large tumor in her chest. Ron returned home and went back to work a few days after

Alyson began chemo, keeping in touch by phone. I stayed while Alyson was in the hospital. Kind friends at Freed-Hardeman took over my classes. At the hospital, I was another pair of ears to listen to what all the many doctors said—all the numerous complicated instructions, all the strange sounding drugs and their frightening side effects. Alyson was such a little trouper—so mature for a two year old. She even handled the IV in her arm without pulling on it.

Finally, after three days of chemo, the tumor in her chest had shrunk enough to allow her to be put to sleep to implant a port in the upper left portion of her chest. This would allow her to be more comfortable. All her medications could be administered without the pain of many needle sticks.

High Hopes on a Nightmarish Trip

Alyson was put on a two-and-one-half-year protocol, a treatment plan referred to by the doctors as a "road map." I remember thinking that cancer is a nightmarish trip with no enjoyable stops along the way. The end of 125 treatments seemed like too much to bear. How could we endure seeing all our baby would have to go through? But there was to be a rainbow at the end of the journey. Alyson's chances of full recovery, not just remission, were 70 percent. The doctor who was handling her case kept emphasizing this magnificent hope for a cure. He said, "We are looking at medicine in the year 2000, now that 1999 is almost over. We are continually learning new methods for treating lymphoma." He gave us faith that this disease in Alyson's body could be conquered. We knew we could all stand the long grueling two-and-one-half years in order to have her whole again. We had such high hopes.

Moon Face

Soon after I returned home from Atlanta, as Debbie and I took our two-mile walk at 6:00 A.M., she asked me about Alyson's chances. I said, "The doctors say her chances of getting totally well are 70 percent. We don't even want to think about that other 30 percent."

During the next seven months Alyson did well. We all prayed before and during every dose of chemo. Bryan and Leanne were very cautious about infections, contagious diseases, and giving exact doses of medication. One of the doctors made the comment that "you need to be a very intelligent parent when your child has lymphoma" because the treatments are so complicated. Several of the chemos were administered at home. Others were given at the Egleston Children's Hospital clinic. Alyson had to go through painful shots, bone marrow checks, and sickness from the chemicals being pumped into her little body. She was hospitalized only three times after the initial diagnosis, usually for a fever.

She still liked to play outside, dance around the room in all kinds of dress-up clothes, paint, and watch her favorite videos.

Except for losing her beautiful brown curls and gaining a "moon face" from the prednisone, a type of steroid, Alyson looked and acted fairly well most of the time. She still liked to play outside, dance around the room in all kinds of dress-up clothes, paint, and watch her favorite videos. When she didn't feel well, she would sit in the big green rocking chair—a gift from loving friends—with her mom, whom she often called Casey, a name she had made up. Alyson enjoyed playing with words, which frequently led her to rename those in her circle of relatives and friends. Her interests were amazing for a two-year-old.

Although Alyson loved playing with her sister when Meghan came home from school, she missed being around her other little friends. So much of the time she did not get to go to Bible class because of chicken pox epidemics, flu, and other childhood diseases that were dangerous to her when her white blood count was low. Leanne made sure they read many Bible stories together and watched Bible videos. Alyson's faith was strong for such a small child. She often said, "God wouldn't want me to do that." Often, on the way to the clinic she sang:

> When I am afraid I will trust in You,
> Trust in You, trust in You.
> When I am afraid I will trust in You,
> God, my heavenly Father.

Relapses Usher in Fading Hopes

Meghan finished her school year the first week of June. The family went on a fun-filled vacation to South Carolina, to a special spot suggested by the hospital. It was near another children's hospital that was fully equipped to take care of any problems Alyson might encounter. She seemed to be doing well. In only a few weeks the worst of the chemo would be over and she would go on a maintenance protocol. She would still have chemo for almost two more years, but the amount would be less. She should feel better. Her hair should grow back. Bryan and Leanne were joyfully looking forward to a great summer. On June 24, 2000, their joy was turned to grief by the cruelty of cancer. Alyson began running a fever. After a trip to the clinic, the blood test revealed that the cancer was back. A relapse. This time the offending cells were in her bloodstream. The lymphoma was now leukemia.

The next seven days were spent in the hospital receiving a new type of chemo. Alyson responded well, but we knew that her chances of complete recovery were now greatly diminished. The doctors said her only hope for a cure was a bone marrow transplant. Members of the immediate family were tested, but there were no matches. Fairfield Hospital in Minneapolis was contacted; they had done many successful transplants. They had the perfect match of cord blood, the blood from a placenta. Young children especially seem to do well with this type of transplant.

On September 10, Alyson was to go to the hospital in Minnesota. She was beginning to look well again. She was in remission. Her hair was beginning to grow back. An apartment had been secured near the hospital. I planned to go with Leanne and Bryan. Bryan's parents, who were retired, would stay in Atlanta with Meghan. Bryan would be in Minneapolis part of the time, and part of the time in Atlanta. He and Meghan would fly to Minneapolis as many weekends as possible, and also during the Thanksgiving holiday. Our calendars were all marked with Meghan's days off, the days I would go, and the days Ron would go. Leanne and Bryan's Bible class gave Meghan and Alyson clothes suitable for a Minnesota winter. Alyson would have to stay

> This time the offending cells were in her bloodstream. The lymphoma was now leukemia.

in an apartment near the hospital for at least four months after the transplant. We were all set. And then cancer, the spoiler, again made its ugly entrance. Alyson relapsed. Two more types of chemo regimens were tried over the next two months, but neither of these put her back into remission. The bone marrow transplant was not possible. Hope was fading.

Make Her Comfortable

Dreams Come True, an organization that grants wishes to severely sick children, had contacted Leanne and Bryan the spring after Alyson's diagnosis. They wanted to fulfill one of her dreams. Alyson wanted to see *Cinderella*. At the time of the offer, with everything going well, Leanne and Bryan had decided to take the family to Disney World in November after Alyson was on main-tenance doses of chemo. It would be a cool time of year and Alyson should be feeling better by then. It was October 27, almost November, but the whole scenario had changed. Cancer was laughingly trying to dash even a child's last wish.

Cancer was laughingly trying to dash even a child's last wish.

The doctors now told us plainly that there was nothing else they could do for Alyson except make her comfortable. We were all devastated. One doctor said she had a small window of time before the cancer completely took over her little body. Leanne mentioned Alyson's wish. The doctor said that arrangements should be made quickly to go to Disney World. A generous friend, Jim, offered to fly us free in his corporate plane. A precious nurse, Ann, offered to go with us—without pay. A place to stay at Give Kids the World Village was secured. Both sets of grandparents, along with Bryan, Leanne, Meghan, Alyson, and Ann, left on Tuesday, October 31, 2000, to fly to Florida. Alyson looked so weak, we all wondered if the trip was a good idea. One doctor thought she shouldn't go, but another thought she could make it. The doctors insisted we take DNR papers with us. I shuddered when I heard what that meant—Do Not Resuscitate. What a horrible thought. This was our baby, and we were saying that if she stopped breathing, she should not be resuscitated. Intellectually, we knew it was the humane thing to do, but our hearts cried "No!"

Mesmerized by Cinderella

When we got to Give Kids the World, Alyson was transformed. She was so thrilled with the magic of the kid-sized village, she even felt like dressing up for the Halloween activities that evening. But that night Alyson vomited many times. Ann, our precious nurse, took care of her, giving her antibiotics and pain medications to keep her as comfortable as possible. By the next morning Alyson was feeling well enough to go to Disney World. We got a wheelchair so Leanne could sit in the chair and hold Alyson as we began to tour the park.

We soon found an information booth. As we were standing in line to inquire about the location of *Cinderella*, Alyson began to vomit. The kind Disney World employee at the information booth immediately took us to find *Cinderella*. When Alyson saw Cinderella from a distance, she was mesmerized. She was allowed to go to the front of the line ahead of many other children. When those in line saw the joy on her face, there was hardly a dry eye to be seen. Strangers in the long line were crying. Alyson's wish was fulfilled.

For three days we toured Disney World, seeing characters that delighted both Meghan and Alyson, riding Dumbo, and seeing *It's a Small World*. In the evenings Alyson loved riding the carousel at Give Kids the World Village. She even ate a few bites during our stay, something she hadn't done in two months. All her food had been given intravenously.

Permission to Go

After returning from Disney World, Alyson lived two weeks. The week after returning, she went to see Disney on Ice. She loved it. At intermission she began to cry. Leanne thought she must be feeling really bad. No, Alyson thought the show was over and that had made her sad.

During the next week she was readmitted to the hospital. She slept much of the time. Strong pain medications made her comfortable. On the morning she died, four couples, both sets of grandparents, and Jody—Leanne and Bryan's minister—were at the hospital. They had spent the night there. About ten minutes before Alyson died, she opened her eyes as if to ask permission to go. Leanne and Bryan said, "It's okay to go, darling. The angels have a party ready for you. Go to the party. We love you." After that she breathed calmly and her short life on earth was over.

God's Lesson?

After the funeral, as Leanne and I sat in a half-dazed state writing thank-you notes, Leanne said, "What do you think God was trying to teach us through this?" I said to my broken-hearted daughter, "I really don't know."

Leanne's question prompted the writing of this book. I still don't know what God was trying to teach us through this absolutely horrible experience. Perhaps He wasn't trying to teach us anything. But I do know what I have learned, and that is what I want to share with you. Whether you have lost a child, a spouse, a parent, or a friend through death, or whether you have had some other loss in your life, such as through divorce, I hope what I have learned may be helpful to you.

Alyson (October 1999) a month before lymphoma diagnosis (Permission for use granted by Olan Mills, July 18, 2006)

Like one who takes off a garment
on a cold day, or like vinegar
on soda, is he who sings songs
to a troubled heart.

Proverbs 25:20

Alyson in the Egleston Hospital garden with
"Tiger Lily," her favorite dog visitor

Chapter 2

Don't Say It!

Don't Say, "It Is Good . . ."

Some things should not be said to those who are grieving. "It's good that . . ." should never begin a sentence in a conversation with a person overcome with grief. I know people were trying to be comforting when they said, "It's good that you know that Alyson has a wonderful home in heaven," but the funeral home was not the proper place for such a statement. It was much too soon. To us there was nothing "good" about Alyson's death. We wanted her there to hold, to hear her talk, to watch her smile. I wanted *her*! My arms cried out to hold her. My ears cried out to hear her sweet voice. My eyes cried out for one more glimpse of her running and jumping into my lap. I knew that in the future I would be comforted by seeing visions of Alyson enjoying being with God and the angels, but now, emotionally, I could not find good in my sorrow.

To a grieving mother, there was nothing good about that precious baby's death.

People also said, "It's good that she isn't suffering anymore." These were people who didn't know how strongly Alyson held onto life even the very last evening she lived, how she had aroused from her pain-medication-induced sleep of several days to play Bingo with the other children at the hospital—just seventeen hours before she died. If you had asked Alyson if she had suffered during the past year, if she had understood the word, she would have surely said, "No." Through her gregarious nature she had found much joy in getting to know the doctors, nurses, and other patients during the year since her diagnosis. She had loved the conversations with all the many visitors. She had delighted in sitting in the playroom at the hospital, petting the dogs that visited, seeing the puppet shows and, yes, winning neat prizes at Bingo.

I Said It; I Regret It!

As I listened to others make statements that were not helpful, I remembered something I had said about thirty years before, a statement I regretted soon after I said it—and even more now. I went with several other women to the home of a friend, Donna, who had lost a two-day-old baby—a baby who had not come home from the hospital.

When we got to Donna's house no one was saying anything. Words felt uncomfortable. The very air felt uncomfortable. Unfortunately, I filled the void with: "It's good that the clothes and things you have here at the house don't seem so personally hers, since she never came home from the hospital." What a foolish statement! To a grieving mother, there was nothing good about that precious baby's death. All her things did seem personal even if she never touched them.

Many years later one of my other friends said how much she regretted not going to see Donna after her baby's death. She said she didn't know what to say. I told her that I had regretted going, because although I didn't know what to say, I said something anyway—the wrong thing. Just going and saying nothing would have been a loving thing to do. I'm sure Donna forgave me for my foolish statement, just as my family and I have forgiven those who made "It is good that . . ." statements to us.

Get Over Missing Her? Never!

One of my students had a miscarriage. She said it hurt so much for people to say, "It's good that you were only thirteen weeks pregnant and not further along." She said, "I loved that baby for thirteen weeks. There's nothing good about losing someone I love."

My friend Debbie lost a sixteen-day-old son to meningitis. Some people said to her, "It's good that you have two other children." She said she wanted to scream, "But they're not him. I want him, too!"

Richard and Barbara, two other faculty members at Freed-Hardeman, lost a sixteen-month-old grandson in 2002. Aaron had a heart transplant when he was only six months old, but died of a breathing problem that was not related to his transplant. According to Richard, the most hurtful thing anyone said to him during the weeks following Aaron's death was: "You'll just have to get over missing him."

I know I will never get over missing Alyson any more than Richard and Barbara will get over missing Aaron. Yes, in time we will be able to experience joy rather than utter sorrow when thinking about our babies, but "get over missing them"?—never! Richard said the most comforting act involved no words at all, but simply another faculty member, Gary, sitting beside him for a long time without saying a word. Our comforting statements during those first freshly wounded days need to be restricted to: "I'm so sorry," "You are in my prayers," "I love you," and "Let me help you by . . ."

You Can't Know!

When my family and I are comforting others, we must remember not to say, "I know just how you feel." We can't even feel the same way some other person feels who lost a three-year-old to cancer. How much more can we not feel like an acquaintance who lost her husband and four of her five children in an automobile accident? Grief is individual, no matter how catastrophic or mild.

"I know just how you feel," one person said. "I just lost my grandmother."

I wanted to yell, "No, you don't know just how I feel! Even if you *just* lost a three-year-old to cancer, you don't know *just* how I feel. We are different people." An acquaintance at a conference my husband, Ron, attended two months after Alyson's death provided an appropriate helpful statement. He said, "Ron, I don't know you very well, but I wanted you to know I have been thinking about you during this difficult time. My twenty-year-old son died of cancer two years ago. I know your grief is not the same as mine, but I feel I have some idea of what you're going through. I just wanted you to know that I care."

God's Will

Here's another stinging statement: "It's God's will. We don't understand because His ways are higher than ours." I didn't want to hear that God willed our beautiful, innocent three-year-old to die. I didn't even want to believe it was God's will. It's true we didn't understand why it happened, but it surely wasn't because God willed her to die. I can accept that He didn't perform a miracle to save her—and oh, how I prayed for a miracle—but to me that is not "His will."

Alan Highers, one of the ministers at the church I attend, preached a sermon about God's will ten months after Alyson's death. He said God's will is never to give us unnecessary pain, although pain comes into our lives. His will is not for people to suffer and to die, but these things happen because we are in a finite world. I was greatly comforted by the sermon. Alan was talking about the God I know.

Good and Perfect Gift

My brother-in-law, Lou Butterfield, wrote the following in a column published in the *Arkansas Gazette* a few days before Alyson died:

The Bible says, "Every good and perfect gift comes from God." It says, "Nothing can separate us from the love of God." So only good things come from God, not the bad.

God did not dream up cancer to whip people into shape. He didn't decide to punish my niece by making her sick. He didn't decide to punish some great wrong done by her parents by taking it out on a three-year-old. If you believe He did, Satan has done a great job pulling the wool over your eyes. Satan is crafty, he is wicked, he doesn't play fair, and he makes his own rules.

The irony is Satan may be winning some of the battles now, but he has already lost the war. He is doomed to eternity in hell, along with those who fall for his lies. The continued irony is when my niece dies her victory will be complete. She will have no more pain, sickness, crying, or suffering. The angels of heaven will come and carry her soul to Paradise, where she will be waiting for Jesus to be sent back to earth to claim all those who are living for Him. She will be reunited with her Christian family. She will be pain free and Satan free. Thank God for the "victory that is in Christ Jesus our Lord."

Just Be There

Although it is meant to help the Christian mourner, saying "it is God's will" brings only more sorrow. Solomon wisely speaks of those who try to say something cheerful to those who are grieving. "Like one who takes off a garment on a cold day, or like vinegar on soda, is he who sings songs to a troubled heart" (Proverbs 25:20). Don't try to cheer up the grieving. Just be there for them. Let them know you love them. Talk isn't always wise or necessary. Job's three friends were kind when they sat with him for seven days without saying a word. They caused Job extreme grief when they began to speak.

In a television interview, Ted Olsen, Solicitor General of the United States, who lost his wife Barbara in one of the plane crashes of the September 11 tragedy said, "In those first few days after one's loved one dies, people gather around you to insulate you from the emotions that are packed so solidly in your body." People do not need to be around you to say anything. They just need to be there.

God Understands Sorrow

"We have to trust in a higher power" is not a helpful statement. It is almost an indictment! Just because we are falling apart with grief does not mean that we aren't trusting in God. It means that we can't stand the thought of being without our beloved family member. We have human feelings—human feelings given to us when God breathed life into us. The Bible tells us our God can experience sadness and sorrow. He understands His created beings.

We were all intellectually aware of our much-sought-after heavenly home, but at the time of our open-wound grief, this awareness was not enough to keep us from writhing in the pain of loss. "We know that if the earthly tent which is our house is torn down, we have a building from God, a house not made with hands" (2 Corinthians 5:1).

> People do not need to be around you to say anything. They just need to be there.

Oh that I were as in months gone by . . .
when the Almighty was yet with me,
and my children were around me.

Job 29:2–5

*Alyson in her backyard fort on a winter day
two months after lymphoma diagnosis*

Chapter 3

Grieving Is Hard Work

Not in Our Family

To our family, death was a stranger. Tragic events, such as the death of a child, didn't happen. Family members lived very long lives. Both my grandmothers lived well into their eighties. One grandfather was ninety-two when he passed away. All my many aunts and uncles were at least sixty-five, most were in their eighties, and some in their nineties when death came. At the time of Alyson's death, my mother was ninety-one and going strong. The death of a child in our family was inexplicable. I had no idea how very hard grieving could be.

I did not know that after a great loss, a person can be drastically changed. Following Alyson's death, I noticed that I was often tired without apparent reason. I did not sleep well. I often woke up in a cold sweat. My blood pressure was normal; it had always been low. I never knew when tears would come. Sometimes the tear-trigger was a song at church, a glance at a picture, a flash of memory—or seemingly, for no reason at all.

License to Cry

I rarely cried at work. I saved my mourning for the privacy of my home or car. When I was in high school, my "prophecy" was that I would be an actress with a star on my door. I am a teacher, which in many ways makes me an actress, but no performance has taken the art of playing a role like not crying every moment during those first few months after returning to work. The only star on my door was the gleam of hope that I could overcome the piercing pain of loss.

Often on my long drives home from visiting student-teachers, I gave myself license to cry and wail. I would scream at the top of my lungs things such as "No!" "Why?" and "I can't stand it. This is too hard, God. Memories are just not enough!" This outrageous behavior in a solemn atmosphere made me feel better. It released pent-up emotions. It

> Sometimes the tear-trigger was a song at church, a glance at a picture, a flash of memory—or seemingly, for no reason at all.

allowed me to face the world—the everyday world that went on as usual, even though many times I felt as if I were not really a part of it anymore. I only pretended to be.

Like Job, who wished for his former life of comfort and family, I wished to return to those wonderfully happy days when Alyson was with us. Job said, "Oh that I were as in months gone by . . . as I was in the prime of my days, when the friendship of God was over my tent; when the Almighty was yet with me, and my children were around me" (Job 29:2–5). Job knew he couldn't go back to the former life, but he still wished.

Lingering Loss

A man whose wife had been killed in a car accident spoke in chapel at Freed-Hardeman University. He told us that he wished he would suddenly wake up from a coma and find her by his side. My family and I wanted to say, "It is morning and the nightmare is over." We found it was not so simple. No matter how many times we woke in the morning, Alyson was not with us. The tragedy of her loss lingered. Eventually, we realized that we had to make a choice—drown our lives in unending sorrow or work to make each day a living memorial to a child who truly enjoyed life; a memorial of joy, caring, and love. We believe morning will come in due time, a morning blessed with the face of the Savior welcoming us to Alyson's home, but for now we must remember to live.

At work I usually answered questions about Alyson and spoke freely about her without emotional outbursts. But then, returning alone to my computer, I often shed a few tears before I could get things together again. And even now, at the most unsuspecting times I occasionally break down.

Once a faculty member spotted a treasured photograph on my desk and said, "What a sweet picture of Alyson!" A flood of my tears descended on him. It is just like the precious little book *Tear Soup* says:

> We just don't know when we will need to make a little more tear soup. Months after a tragedy we can keep the tear soup in the freezer for a while, but then we need to take it out again and taste its bitterness once more.

Mourning Customs

I wonder if we have lost something by not allowing ourselves to mourn in public as the Hebrews did. They went about wailing and mourning forty days after a loss. Their practice was probably healthier than ours is. In our culture, after about three weeks we are expected to no longer cry in public. Actually, after a great loss we are probably numb for those first three weeks. Our daughter Leanne likened our feelings during those first weeks after Alyson's death to those of a deer staring into headlights; he knows he should run, but he is too stunned to move.

For some of us, tears are even closer to the surface after many weeks have passed. Barbara Bush, when writing about her daughter's death—three-year-old Robin—says, "For one who allowed no tears before her death, I fell apart, and time after time during the next six months, George would put me together again."

Two months after Alyson's death, I still refused to lead prayer in our ladies' Bible class. I have led prayers for years, but I know my limits. After my father died I had no trouble resuming my role as a leader among the women. I loved my father dearly, but he had lived a full and wonderful life. He was ready to go. Alyson was also ready to go, but she was so young and had lived so little. Her passing has been much harder to accept. I believe we need to let people grieve in their own way. I knew I would fall apart in Bible class if I led the prayer. I didn't feel I should put others through that emotional trauma, even though I know my Christian sisters would have understood. I felt no guilt about realizing my limits.

Sweet Memories

My diary entry on April 5, 2001, Alyson's birthday:

This would have been Alyson's fourth birthday. I knew it would be a hard day at work. I got cards from several kind people who remembered that this would have been her special day. I had not gone to the cemetery since November when she had been buried. I went today. The marker had just been put there. It was a heart with her name and date of birth and date of death—oh, they are so close together. The people who placed the marker had put red flowers in the vase that is part of the marker. It was a nice thing to do, but I will replace them with pink ones—Alyson's favorite color.

> The Hebrews went about wailing and mourning forty days after a loss.

I didn't mention to anyone in the office that this would have been Alyson's birthday. It was my long day. I had to teach for four-and-one-half hours, observe a student-teacher, advise some students, and go to a meeting. I asked God to give me strength to get through this day—special strength for this intense day of memory. My classes went well, as did my other activities.

But when I got home I gave myself permission to wail. It was okay; I was alone. Ron had an overnight meeting in Nashville. Crying was replaced with happy memories of other birthdays. I remembered Alyson's second birthday at our house, complete with a big sunflower cake and little lady bug and bee cakes all around the flower. It was not just a birthday celebration for Alyson, but for Meghan and my grandson, David, too. It was so much fun. We have pictures of everyone eating out in the carport and opening presents in the driveway. Last year it was a Little Mermaid cake at her house in Atlanta.

I know there is no time in heaven, so there will be no birthdays, but like Meghan I believe there must be one wonderful continual party for a curly haired little girl named Alyson.

New Life among Silent Markers

Visiting the grave of a loved one brings comfort to many, but it has always been the most difficult thing I do during the grieving process. The solemn stillness of rows of silent markers attest to the reality of death. In contrast, pictures of Alyson and things she touched remind me of life—the three-and-one-half years of a beautiful little person who lived life to its fullest and still lives in heaven.

Then one day when I went to the cemetery alone to take flowers—pink ones with a tiny stuffed bear attached—I experienced a feeling of renewal. This was not because I saw "Alyson Kate Black" carved in the cold, heart-shaped stone and the much-too-close-together dates underneath, but because I saw next to her grave a beautiful expression of life. In a little nest on the ground were four quarter-size speckled eggs.

Suddenly a mother killdeer began giving the performance of a lifetime. In an attempt to protect her soon-to-be-born babies, she was fluttering—half-flying, half-running—feigning a broken wing, trying to get the human intruder to chase her. I said aloud, as if she could understand, "I won't hurt your babies. I'm glad you put them here." I was happy because eggs were a sign of new life.

Baby birds have always made me smile. We had once had a killdeer lay her eggs in a small flower garden in our front yard. I had carefully protected them, even letting our grass grow high so the lawnmower would not disturb the protective mother. We were fortunate enough to see the eggs hatch and watch the fuzzy little babies run all around and then disappear into the woods nearby.

We Would Lay Down Our Lives

The actions of the killdeer reminded me how we would all have protected Alyson if only we could have had the power. Just as the mother bird was willing to lay down her life for her young, any person in our family would have done the same for Alyson. Others would have also been willing to give up their lives for her. As Jody, the minister at her funeral, said, "If some member of the church could take Alyson's place, the line of volunteers would reach for miles through Atlanta."

I was also happy that the killdeer had decided to lay her eggs near this particular grave, because Alyson would have thought it was a very neat thing to have baby birds running all around near her special plot of land. She would have giggled and giggled at the thought. Perhaps the bird will sense that this is a safe and peaceful place for new lives to begin and return next year.

O You who hear prayer,
To You all men come.

Psalm 65:2

Chapter 4

No One Should Tell You How to Grieve

Free of Rules

Some of Leanne's acquaintances worried about her because she did not cry at all in public. They were afraid she was denying the loss and not allowing herself to grieve. Leanne's close friends understood that her grieving was deep inside rather than outward, especially in public—something like her own mother's grieving.

Bryan did not want to go to a memorial service at the hospital for all the children who had died during the previous year. He felt he was expected to go because he was Alyson's father and she was one of those being remembered. I told him he should do whatever he felt like doing, that no one should tell him how he should grieve or judge him for the way he chose to grieve. Grieving should be an individual activity, free of rules.

Leanne says some people are "tricklers" and some are "wailers." Tricklers cry and grieve little by little. Wailers cry big, and each wailing session lasts a very long time. Leanne said that Bryan and I are tricklers, but she is a wailer. When she starts, she can't stop. Everyone needs to grieve—cry or not cry—in his or her own way.

Be Sensitive

In her book, Barbara Bush: A Memoir, the former first lady says that she went to play golf the day after her daughter, Robin, died of leukemia. She continues by saying that she is sure others did not understand. "I, for one, was numb," she writes. At a time like this, understanding is not important; caring is. After Alyson's death, hitting something might have seemed good, even if the target were a golf ball.

Leo Buscaglia, author and lecturer on loving relationships, once talked about a contest he judged. He was looking for someone who knew what to do to help those who were grieving. The winner was a four-year-old boy whose elderly neighbor had recently lost his wife. When the boy saw the man in the yard, he went out and climbed into his lap and just sat there. When his mother asked him what he had said to the neighbor, the little boy said, "Nothing, I just helped him cry." Sometimes all we need is the quietness of someone helping us cry.

Bill Cosby performed a comedy act soon after his son's tragic murder. He said he was sure some would not understand, but he felt he was honoring his son by doing his best at his job. Others don't have to understand why we express our grief as we do.

The next time you are Christmas shopping in a mall, remember that some of the ordinary-looking people that you meet are grieving. Be extra kind to everyone. Just a month after Alyson's death, Leanne and I were walking through a mall trying to look for presents for Meghan and thinking how oblivious we often are to the pain in others' hearts.

Tricklers cry and grieve little by little. Wailers cry big, and each session lasts a very long time. Everyone needs to grieve—cry or not cry—in her own way.

Whoever then humbles himself
as this child, he is the greatest
in the kingdom of heaven.

Matthew 18:4

Alyson at 18 months
all dressed up with sister Meghan

Chapter 5

A Child's Perspective Can Be a Blessing

"Out of the mouths of babes and sucklings hast thou ordained strength because of thine enemies, that thou mightest still the enemy and the avenger" (Psalm 8:2 KJV)

The Bereaved Sibling

In *Sunrise*, a column in our local newspaper, Don Harold Lawrence wrote: "The bereaved sibling is often one of the most overlooked and neglected grievers in society . . . [He or she] looses a friend, playmate, sidekick, confidant, source of encouragement, rival, and role model." Lawrence also said that many times the child loses the emotional support of parents and other adults in his or her life for a time because these important people are focused so much on the child who has died.

Children are sometimes told to be strong for their parents. What they really need is someone to say, "We know you're hurting. We're here for you." Barbara Bush says that after Robin's death she heard her seven-year-old son, George, tell a friend he couldn't leave his mother and go play because she needed him. He had decided that his job was to make his mother feel better after the death of his sister.

Sticker Pox and Baby Tackles

We were all concerned about Alyson's seven-year-old sister, Meghan. Although they were four years apart, they were very good friends. They both loved imaginative play. Once when we were on a three-hour trip with fourteen-month-old Alyson and five-year-old Meghan, we gave them two big pages of very small stickers. After a few minutes, we looked and there sat Alyson with tiny round stickers all over her chubby little body. They both giggled and yelled, "Sticker pox!" Other times they tore up tiny pieces of paper to make "soup" and pretended to feed all the toys before their little charges had to go to school. One day Alyson was lying on the floor with her doll on her stomach. When Meghan and I walked in, Alyson said in a desperate tone, "I don't know what I'm going to do with

> What children really need is someone to say, "We know you're hurting. We're here for you."

her. This baby tackles me all the time." Meghan and I roared with laughter.

After Alyson was diagnosed with lymphoma, she and Meghan often played doctor. Alyson was always "Dr. Reid." We don't know where she got this name because it did not belong to any of her myriad of physicians. Meghan was the mother bringing one of the dolls to Dr. Reid, who always made the baby well. I often just sat back and watched those two beautiful imaginations intertwine.

Meghan was always so good to Alyson. One of my favorite pictures is of Meghan and Alyson playing a game on the computer. With the effects of the chemo in full force, Alyson's head is very bald. Meghan had just reached over and kissed the top of that very sweet bald head when I snapped the picture. Many other pictures show the girls dancing around happily together or enjoying a common laugh.

A Participant in the Process

Many times Alyson was very ill tempered because of a combination of the drugs, her aggressive personality, and just being two years old—going on three. Meghan was very tolerant of Aly's outbursts. She patiently put up with more than most siblings would have. These sisters shared a true oneness of spirit.

Because of their close friendship, we were concerned about Meghan and how she, being so young, would handle great loss. No one in Meghan's family had ever died. She still had two great-grandmothers and both sets of grandparents. And now the catastrophic loss of her little sister. Immediately after Alyson's death, Meghan had acted as if nothing had happened. It was her way of coping. At first she said she didn't want to see Alyson in the casket at the funeral home. We hoped she would change her mind, but we wanted her to make her own decision. We felt the act of viewing her sister's body would help take away some of the mystery—that it would help her have some closure in this unbelievably dreadful experience.

After being at the funeral home for a while, Meghan decided to view Alyson's body. That decision evoked many questions about death. Later that same evening, Meghan began taking some of her young friends visiting the funeral home over to the casket. It was good for Meghan to have a part in this exceptionally trying time for her family.

Someone Here to Hug

Although we at first worried about Meghan, we found that she had a wonderful picture of Alyson—of Alyson in heaven. She wanted to know if Alyson would stay the same age she was when she died. We had never really thought about that. We said we didn't really know, but she probably would still think like she did as a three-year-old. Meghan also said she really wished Jesus would come back now so that we could all be together in heaven. Secretly we had wished that, too. Meghan never said she wished Alyson could come back to earth. She pictured her in heaven without cancer and having such a marvelous time. She wouldn't want to spoil Alyson's fantastic new life. Meghan helped us to put away our selfishness and capture this precious picture, too.

Meghan said, "I know that, but I need someone here to hug." Yes, that's the way I feel, too.

44

Two weeks before Christmas, a short time after Alyson died, we took Meghan and her parents to Cancun, Mexico. We all needed to go to a warm pleasant place far from anyone we knew, just for a short time, to help clear our heads and prepare ourselves for the reality of living without our beloved Alyson. As we looked at the beautiful turquoise water, Meghan reminded us that Alyson had a much more beautiful beach and much more beautiful water in heaven. What a blessing it was to have her describing what a good time Alyson must be having, just as if she were on a beautiful, everlasting vacation—which she is.

On a tour bus in Cancun, a lady sitting near Meghan asked her if she had any brothers or sisters. I felt my heart being torn into pieces as Meghan answered, "I used to." The lady continued, "What happened to them?" "I had a sister," Meghan said. "She had cancer. She was lots of fun . . ." And she continued to tell the stranger the good things about her little sister. My heart broke for her. Later, Leanne was saying to Meghan that Alyson would always be her sister, but that she now lived in heaven. Meghan said, "I know that, but I need someone here to hug." Yes, that's the way I feel, too.

Comfort of a Seven-Year-Old

At Christmas, a little over a month after Alyson's death, while we were feeling intense sorrow because Alyson was not with us to share the joy of the season, Meghan was talking about how much more wonderful holidays must be in heaven—more beautiful trees, more wonderful presents, more delicious food. We didn't try to correct any of her seven-year-old misconceptions because the things she said about heaven comforted her as well as us.

Because Alyson was very outgoing and assertive, Meghan also said that by now she had probably convinced Gabriel that he should let her blow his horn. She had just kept talking to him about it until he let her. Yes, we thought she probably had, too.

On April 5, which would have been Alyson's fourth birthday, Meghan asked Leanne, "Do they have confetti in heaven?" Leanne said, "I don't really know. Why?" Meghan said, "I can just imagine the angels throwing confetti all over Alyson and saying 'Happy Birthday!'" Are there birthdays in heaven? Probably not, since there is no time, but to a seven-year-old it was a beautiful picture of happiness.

A Place to Call Home

Meghan has helped us all to determine even more resolutely that we will serve God faithfully so we may one day join Alyson.

Six months after Alyson's death, Meghan's teacher asked her pupils to draw a picture of their families. Meghan's picture showed her mother, her dad, and herself standing in a row near the bottom of the paper. In the upper right-hand portion was a small child with curly hair walking on a golden street near a large gate made of what appeared to be pearls. Alyson was still a member of the family; she always will be. She just lives in a different place, a place all her family members are also making elaborate, day-by-day plans to call home.

Eight months after Alyson's death, Meghan told her mother she thought they should get some walkie-talkies so they could "keep up with Daddy" in the mall. Looking pensive, Meghan said, "I wish we had walkie-talkies that could talk for a really long ways—I mean a really long ways, like to heaven. I know there's no such thing, but I'd really like to talk to Alyson. I'd really like to hear about all that she's been doing."

Meghan often makes us laugh as she recounts how happy Alyson is in her new home with Jesus. Her beautiful childlike spirit has comforted us. Although Meghan sincerely misses her sister, she has been the first one of us to truly rejoice in Alyson's gift of an eternal home in heaven. Meghan has helped us all to determine even more resolutely that we will serve God faithfully so we may one day join Alyson in the glory of her heavenly Father.

He makes His sun rise on the evil
and on the good, and sends rain
on the just and on the unjust.

Matthew 5: 45

Alyson enjoying a show with Mom at
Disneyworld, November 2000

Chapter 6

Life Is Not Always Fair

A Good Lesson to Learn

When our children, Brian, Keith, and Leanne, were still at home they were responsible for doing certain chores. The chores usually rotated so no one got stuck every day with the one he or she disliked the most. When the children became teens, they often had activities such as play practice or athletic practice that kept them after school. The chores still had to be done, so the child or children at home had to do extra work. At first they complained. I often heard: "This is not fair!" I had a standard reply: "This is a good lesson for you to learn because life is not always fair. If you are an employee and someone gets sick, you may have to do his job. Maybe it doesn't seem fair, but that's reality. So go on and get the dishes done, even though it is his (her) night."

Our daughter-in-law, Kay, an accomplished pianist, had surgery to remove a tumor on the auditory nerve near her brain in February after Alyson was diagnosed with lymphoma in November. The surgery was very delicate and serious. We prayed and prayed that she would be completely healed. Kay has recovered but she lost her hearing in one ear. Is it fair for a musician to have this great loss? Is it fair for all of us to have to endure sorrow for Kay's loss, as well as the sorrow over Alyson's illness? Life is not fair.

I read about a mother who left her child in a hot car for seven hours while she worked at a fast food restaurant? The child died because of the parent's negligence. Leanne and Bryan had done everything right to prevent Alyson's death, and yet she did not live. Why the same fate for inappropriate and appropriate behaviors? Life is not fair.

Why?

Why did Alyson have to be overtaken with lymphoma? Statistically, one in one million two-year-old-white American females contract lymphoma. Why Alyson?

My mother, who was ninety-one when Alyson died, hardly realized it was Christmas. Though her body is strong, her mind fails to give her correct messages. Her short-term memory is practically nonexistent. Alyson would have whole heartedly enjoyed every second of the holiday playing with Meghan. Was it fair for her Christmases with her earthly family to be over? Was it fair for Alyson who looked so healthy to have lymphoma? Was it fair to relapse with leukemia when she had a seventy percent chance of recovery? Was it fair for a perfect cord blood match to be found but for her never to be in remission long enough to use it? Was it fair for everything to seem to fall into place so perfectly for the stay in Minnesota for the bone marrow transplant, and for Alyson to never get to make the trip? Was it fair for her to die at the age of three?

Goodness and Adversity

Just as I can ask those questions, can I not also ask others? Is it fair that I have had reasonable health for more than sixty years while others suffer throughout their lives? Is it fair that I had three healthy children who were rarely sick? Is it fair that I was born into a middle-class family in the United States while others are born into destitute poverty in third-world countries? Is it fair that Leanne and Bryan were able to have two beautiful daughters, even if they were only allowed to keep one for three years, while some people are never able to have any children? Is it fair that my husband and I, as well as our three children, were blessed to grow up in loving Christian homes, while many others find themselves in cruel and abusive situations? Was it fair that Alyson tolerated all the chemotherapy so well, allowing her to live for a year after diagnosis, while other children die a few days into their treatments?

> Is it fair for us to have to endure sorrow? Life is not fair.

Fairness works both ways. What did we do to deserve the good things in our lives? Job said it best when he spoke to his wife who had encouraged him to curse God,

"Shall we indeed accept good from God and not accept adversity?" (Job 2:10).

A Precious Gift

I suppose Jody Vickery, the preacher at the Campus Church of Christ in Duluth, Georgia, helped us the most with our dilemma of fairness. When speaking at Alyson's funeral he said, "It is not the length of one's life that determines the usefulness of that life. It is the way a life is lived." Alyson had brought joy to numerous people through her gregarious personality that had a way of grabbing you and sucking her giggling little self under your skin. Some people never bring that much joy to others, even if they live an entire century. Even a long life is short in God's eyes: "As for the days of our life, they contain seventy years, or if due to strength, eighty years, yet their pride is but labor and sorrow; for soon it is gone and we fly away" (Psalm 90:10). Alyson was spared most of the trouble and sorrow of life. She found peace and safety in the arms of Jesus. In the process of living her short life, she left us a precious gift.

He is great enough to see us through "momentary, light affliction" which is "producing for us an eternal weight of glory far beyond all comparison."

Some people just come through our lives to bring us something—
a gift, a blessing, a lesson we need to learn,
and that's why they're here.
They teach us about love, and giving, and caring;
that was their gift to you.
They maybe didn't need to stay longer than that,
give you a gift and then they were free to move on, a special soul.
You'll have that gift forever.
—Anonymous

"I again saw under the sun that the race is not to the swift, and the battle is not to the warriors, and neither is bread to the wise, nor wealth to the discerning, nor favor to men of ability; for time and chance overtake them all" (Ecclesiastes 9:11).

We have to realize that some things in our lives seem to be there by chance. Though God is present in every aspect of our lives, He allows Satan to roam freely. Can we blame Satan for whatever it was that caused Alyson to have leukemia? I don't know. Was it by chance that she had a gene that was susceptible to this disease? I don't know. God never promises us we won't have problems. He only promises that He is great enough to see us through "momentary, light affliction" which is "producing for us an eternal weight of glory far beyond all comparison" (2 Corinthians 4:17). Sometimes we are allowed to walk calmly by "quiet waters." Other times we trudge through "the valley of the shadow of death." He has promised to be with us so that we "fear no evil" (Psalm 23).

No Promise of Fairness

When I heard some ladies at church talking about how much fun they would have taking their grandchildren to Disney World, I wanted to say, "How would you like to take your grandchild to Disney World and know it was the last time she would ever go? How would you like to know that it might be the last thing she would ever see?" How was it fair for them to have grandchildren to have fun with them when one of mine had just died?

Thankfully, I didn't say any of those things. Just because I was hurting, there was no reason to hurt others by lashing out at their joy. We have never been promised that life will be fair.

Jeremiah wondered about the fairness of God in dealing with the wicked.

> "Righteous art Thou, O Lord, that I would plead my case with Thee; indeed I would discuss matters of justice with Thee: Why has the way of the wicked prospered? Why are all those who deal in treachery at ease?" (Jeremiah 12:1).

Job also questioned God's fairness in allowing the children of the wicked to live when his had died.

> "Why do the wicked still live, continue on, also become very powerful? Their descendants are established with them in their sight . . . Neither is the rod of God on them . . . They spend their days in prosperity, And suddenly they go down to Sheol. And they say to God, 'Depart from us! We do not even desire the knowledge of Thy ways'" (Job 21:7–14).

Even David struggled with the prosperity and health of the wicked. "I was envious of the arrogant, as I saw the prosperity of the wicked. For there are no pains in their death; and their body is fat" (Psalm 73:3–4).

On the other hand, David wondered why God even takes note of man, the creature He has made. "O Lord, what is man that Thou dost take knowledge of him? Or the son of man, that Thou dost think of him?" (Psalm 144:3). Can we, as David did, look at both sides of fairness?

Just because I was hurting, there was no reason to hurt others by lashing out at their joy.

Look not every man on his
own things, but every man also
on the things of others.

Philippians 2:4

*Alyson at her great-grandmother's
house, summer 1999*

Chapter 7

Giving to Others Helps with One's Own Grief

Cookies and Locks of Love

When I returned to Atlanta just a few weeks after Alyson died, Leanne suggested that Meghan and I make cookies to take to Egleston Hospital to give to the nurses who had been so kind to all of us. It was good for Meghan to have an opportunity to give back to those who had given to all of us, especially to Alyson. It was eerie for Bryan, Leanne, Meghan, and me to get off the elevator and walk down the hall—the one with the aquarium—on the third floor again, this time without Alyson. But it was good to see some of those who had made our little one's life happier, especially during those last two months. We were especially glad to see Ann, the precious nurse who had accompanied us to Disney World during Aly's last few weeks.

Leanne, Meghan, and our daughter-in-law, Gina, let their hair grow long to give to the Leukemia/Lymphoma Society. The organization that accepts the hair is called Locks of Love. During the summer of 2001, Meghan's hair had already grown enough to have the ten-inch donation that is required. She was very pleased to have a short hair cut so that she could help other children and teens who lose their hair due to chemotherapy.

Sharing Time, Prayers, and Books "In Memory"

I have been amazed how Leanne began immediately to minister to others who were having difficulties. Within the first month she had already taken food to a mother who was hurt in an automobile accident, and helped clean and sort through rubble in freezing temperatures when a friend's house burned.

In a special way, we have all found solace in praying for children being treated for cancer on the third floor of Egleston Hospital. We knew many who were still going through treatments several months after we no longer were fighting that battle.

At Christmas Meghan wanted to choose and take presents to the nurses and doctors who treated Alyson. She used her allowance she had been saving. Every gift was small, but carefully chosen based on her knowledge of the personality and traits of each doctor or nurse. Her gifts were truly from a child's grateful heart.

For Christmas 2001 I made a small tree for Alyson. It was covered with tiny crystal, silver, and crocheted angels I had collected during the year since her death. In 2000 I couldn't put up a tree of any kind. It was too soon. Now I have the traditional large family tree that I usually decorate, in addition to Alyson's little one. The "presents" for Alyson are books given by family members for the playroom at Egleston Hospital. I know Alyson, now that she is safely in God's arms and cancer-free, would think it was great to share her books with children with cancer.

For what would have been Alyson's fifth birthday, Leanne and Bryan invited their close friends over for a special dinner. Guests were asked to bring toys and videos for Egleston Hospital's playroom. A large number of sturdy toys, games, and videos were collected. Alyson is never forgotten because her memory is kept fresh by our helping children who are undergoing similar difficulties associated with cancer treatment.

> Alyson is never forgotten because her memory is kept fresh by our helping children who are undergoing similar difficulties.

Many are the plans in a man's heart,
but the counsel of the Lord,
it will stand.

Proverbs 19:21

Alyson and her sister, Meghan,
on the beach in Florida, summer 1999

Chapter 8

God Hears Our Prayers, but Gives His Answers, Not Ours

An Answer We Do Not Understand

We often hear people say, "It's an answer to prayer," especially when the conversation is about someone recovering from a dreaded illness or about the birth of a child. Did you ever hear anyone say "It's an answer to prayer" when a child dies? But it is. It is an answer, although we don't understand it. We know that "the effectual fervent prayer of a righteous man availeth much" (James 5:16 KJV). I know that many thousands of righteous people all over the world were praying daily for Alyson. One of my colleagues at Freed-Hardeman said after Alyson's death: "I just can't believe she didn't get well. I really thought she'd be here telling her story of recovery for all to hear. I prayed for her every day on my way to work, and so many others did, too. I know God heard our prayers, but . . ." He couldn't go on from there.

I know God heard our prayers concerning Alyson, because I believe in His promises, but He didn't answer them in the way we wanted. When our children ask for candy and we tell them they should eat their dinner instead, they are not usually happy. We have not granted their request no matter how nicely and sincerely they have asked, because we know what is best for them. We must always believe that "God causes all things to work together for good to those who love God, to those who are called according to His purpose" (Romans 8:28). We certainly don't understand how Alyson's death could work for our good. We don't have to understand. We just have to believe that God is just, fair, caring, and good. Matthew 7:7-12 says, "Ask . . . seek . . . knock." We did, but the answer was no. What we were given didn't seem like a good gift. It felt like a gift of coal on Christmas rather than a present. After Alyson's death, I sometimes felt resentment, surprisingly not at God, but at the whole awful situation.

> God heard our prayers concerning Alyson. I believe in His promises, but He didn't answer them in the way we wanted.

Grace Sufficient

We don't know why Alyson lived only three years. Perhaps God was saving us and her from some greater tragedy later in her life. Physical death is devastating, but it is nothing to compare with spiritual death. What if Alyson had lived, never to become a Christian? What if her death had left us no beautiful picture of her in heaven, because of the way she had lived her life? Only God knows what her life would have been like. In our frail human wisdom, we see her growing up as just the kind of person God would want His child to be. That may be a true picture, or it may be a totally fake snapshot. When Paul entreated God to take away his affliction, God answered, "My grace is sufficient for you" (2 Corinthians 12:9). We must also accept God's grace, believing in His omnipotence in all things, even if a child's life is not spared.

We had many plans for Alyson—to go to Minnesota to be cured, to go to kindergarten, to finish high school and college, to get married. "Many are the plans in a man's heart, but the counsel of the Lord, it will stand" (Proverbs 19:21). Faith is trusting God's wisdom and purpose—and not our own—even when we want to question and argue with the decision of the Ruler of all of Creation.

When My Heart Is Faint

Jesus is described as a "man of sorrows, and acquainted with grief" (Isaiah 53:3). God certainly heard Jesus as He prayed for the cup to be taken from Him, but God did not grant the request. There was no other way to save sinful mankind. He said no to His precious Son whom He loved with all His heart. Just because God says no to us does not mean that He doesn't love us.

Even the apostle Paul pleaded with God to take away his "thorn in the flesh" to make things different in his life. "Concerning this I entreated the Lord three times that it might depart from me. And He has said to me, 'My grace is sufficient for you, for power is perfected in weakness'" (2 Corinthians 12:8–9).

As Job we can say, "Though He slay me, I will hope in Him" (Job 13:15).

And with David we can say, "From the end of the earth I call to Thee, when my heart is faint; lead me to the rock that is higher than I" (Psalm 61:2).

Notes

For momentary, light affliction
is producing for us an eternal weight
of glory far beyond all comparison.

2 Corinthians 4:17

*Alyson and Nana at Give Kids the World Village in
Orlando, Florida, three weeks before Alyson's death*

Chapter 9

Life: Never the Same, but Good Again

"That's My Job!"

When I look at pictures of my grandchildren, Alyson always seemed to be in my lap or tucked under my arm. She always found a way to be close to me as much as possible. When my husband, affectionately dubbed PopPop, would ask Alyson if she wanted to go somewhere with him and Meghan, she would say, "No, Meghan can go with you. That's her job. I'll stay here and play with Nana. That's my job." That part of my life—playing with Alyson—will never be the same again. I'm thankful I have beautiful memories of those wonderful times together—memories that can always bring warm feelings of a three-year-old tucked gently under my arm.

During the week of April 5, 2001, when Alyson would have had her fourth birthday, Leanne, Bryan, and Meghan flew from Atlanta to Washington State to a place they had never been. They went to visit Leanne's aunt and uncle, whom she had seen only a few times. They were able to use buddy passes that were given to them to help with flights to Minnesota for the Alyson's bone marrow transplant. Now they were being used to help rebuild their family, not to fill the vacuum left by Alyson's absence, but to strengthen new relationships as a family of three. On Alyson's birthday, Leanne told her Aunt Gwen that their little family needed to be alone all day. Her aunt understood. They spent the day together remembering Alyson and continuing to share an enjoyable time as a different family. It was good to be in a place where Alyson's memories were in their hearts, but not visible in every room or shouting from every piece of backyard playground equipment.

"For These Few Years . . . I Am Thankful"

Before Leanne was married, she told a friend a philosophy of her upbringing: "When things went wrong we learned to cry, wash our faces, and go on with our lives." It isn't so simple when something as catastrophic as the death of a child is concerned, but the principle still applies. With God's help we can go on with our lives. Life will never be the same again, but it can be good again. It is not what we had wished for, but still good.

When Alyson relapsed in June, I think Alyson's father, Bryan, said it best: "No matter what happens, I can never say that I wished we had never had her for our daughter. I am thankful even for these few years as her father."

I also know my life has been enriched by having her for three years as a precious granddaughter.

Gerald Sittser said in *A Grace Disguised*:

> I did not get over the loss of my loved ones; rather, I absorbed the loss into my life, like soil receives decaying matter, until it became a part of who I am. Sorrow took up permanent residence in my soul and enlarged it. I learned gradually that the deeper we plunge into suffering, the deeper we can enter into a new, and different, life—life no worse than before and sometimes better. A willingness to face the loss and to enter into the darkness is the first step we must take.

Fall into the Pain

I believe I learned this "first step" in another situation I had faced. When I had three heart surgeries in less than two months, I experienced more pain than I could ever have imagined. Even morphine didn't take the agony away. I complained to a nurse named Myrtle. She gave me very wise advice that I have used in other situations, not just those involving physical pain. She said, "Honey, you're fighting against the pain. Don't do that. Fall into it."

When Alyson died, I remembered that advice. I fell into grief. I did not try to fight against it. As Sittser said, "A willingness to face the loss and to enter into the darkness is the first step we must take."

"If you have run with footmen and they have tired you out, then how can you compete with horses? If you fall down in a land of peace, how will you do in the thicket of the Jordan?" (Jeremiah 12:5). Little problems like physical suffering from surgery may prepare us for the unthinkably difficult times such as the death of a child. God never gives us a reason for unfaithfulness, because He is always faithful, and we are made in His image.

Eggs, Strawberries, and Flowers

Every time I crack an egg, I think of Alyson. She, Meghan, and I often cooked together. Alyson always wanted to crack the egg. Meghan didn't mind. She liked the less messy jobs, like measuring the flour. Surprisingly, Alyson was an expert at egg cracking—not one bit of shell in the bowl. It always seemed like an amazing feat for such a young child.

When I see strawberries I think of Alyson. How she loved them! Ironically, she preferred healthful foods—broccoli, salads, tomatoes, strawberries—over candy and other sweets. She enjoyed going to Italian restaurants, where we always got special treatment when the server noticed Alyson's bald head and pale face. Our little vegetable eater quickly devoured extra bowls of cut-up tomatoes and black olives.

Flowers remind me of Alyson. She loved them so. Leanne and I dried flowers from Alyson's funeral and hung them upside down in the garage. I was amazed how pretty they looked in May—the first time I had the courage to go and look at them. I put some dried roses, interspersed with some kind of little purple flowers, in a vase in the house. I was surprised how the fragrance remained even after drying. The sweet smell from these blossoms reminded me of Alyson. When she entered a room, you knew she was there. She provided her own type of fragrance to every area—whether she was in a good or bad mood. Leanne had once said of Alyson's aggressive personality: "She surely could be a dictator of a small country."

Tomorrow's Possibilities

Sometimes—after Alyson's death—it seemed wrong to feel real happiness, to laugh. It almost seemed as if I were shrouding her memory. How could I laugh again without the inner feeling of sadness? Linda Richman said in *I'd Rather Laugh,*

> I learned we can withstand a lot of pain and loss and not just survive, but rise above it. No matter how sad you are today, happiness and laughter, and even joy, are distinct possibilities for tomorrow, or if not tomorrow, for the day after that.

For my healing, I enlarged many of our grandchildren's pictures, including some of Alyson's. Many were snapshots I had taken. I covered one of our den walls with them. I want to see all my grandchildren's faces—all eight of them. One of them I can now see only in photographs, but I intend to see these pictures every day. Some grandparents say they have a hard time looking at pictures of their grandchildren who have died. Sometimes I cry when I look at pictures of Alyson because I miss her so much, but most of the time I smile, because I know she is still alive, as alive as ever in her heavenly home.

Gift of Memories

I teach children's literature. Lois Lowry's book, *The Giver,* is a story about a mythical land where there are no emotions, no pain, no colors, and no memories. Only one person, the Receiver, is given the "gift of memory." Memories truly are gifts. They can make a person extremely sad or tremendously happy. If I had no memories of Alyson, my life would lack a wealth of happiness, although those memories also bring floods of tears. I can say with Paul, "I thank my God in all my remembrance of you" (Philippians 1:3). George Bush, Sr. expressed my sentiments in a letter to his mother about his daughter, Robin, who died of leukemia, "She is still with us. We need her and yet we have her. We can't touch her and yet we can feel her."

God says that any trouble we have in this life better prepares us for the wonderful life that is promised.

> For momentary, light affliction is producing for us an eternal weight of glory far beyond all comparison, while we look not at the things which are seen, but at the things which are not seen; for the things which are seen are temporal, but the things which are not seen are eternal (2 Corinthians 4:17–18).

Our finite minds have difficulty comprehending that the death of a child could be a "momentary, light affliction," but our finite minds also have difficulty comprehending heaven.

Life for Living, Not Just Surviving

R. Stafford North wrote in *The Christian Chronicle*: "Hope is our helmet that protects us against the blows that come our way." We wish we never had to wear the helmet of hope, but we are thankful that God makes it available for us.

I decided, as did Bryan and Leanne, that we had to make a choice. Either curl up and die emotionally and spiritually, or make the most of the time we have before we join our loved one in heaven. Many people choose the former. It would be easy to do, so very easy to do—just to forget life. It is much harder to live fully after a tragedy.

In the novel *Desperate Measures* by David Morrell, the main character, Matt—who has lost a son to cancer—begins to drink heavily. He experience conflict with his wife, has a nervous breakdown, and becomes so depressed he decides to commit suicide. In this book, Morrell reflects many of the occurrences of his own life when his son died of cancer. Another book tells of a father who has to be cared for by others for the rest of his life because he can't cope with the loss of his son.

In a serious episode of a popular sitcom, the husband in the family was mysteriously missing for days. The wife made the following insightful statement: "When I go to the grocery store, somebody on the outside is busy being me, but somebody on the inside is busy missing him." She expressed exactly what our family felt for several months. We will always miss Alyson, but the "somebody" on the inside must reconcile with the "somebody" on the outside, so that we can once again feel that life is good for living, not just for surviving.

> God says that any trouble we have in this life better prepares us for the wonderful life that is promised.

I have decided not even to think about "getting over" Alyson's death. I will be sad when she should have started kindergarten, begun high school, got married, had children. I will never get over it. I will live through it—I mean fully live. I will bless her cheerful memory by remembering, but living.

With good will render service,
as to the Lord, and not to men, knowing
that whatever good thing each one does,
this he will receive back from the Lord.

Ephesians 6:7–8

Alyson sitting on the deck
in Florida condo, summer 1999

Chapter 10

Reflections of Jesus: Those Who Ease Your Grief

Looking into the faces of those who ease our grief is like looking into a reflection of Jesus. The following is a list of kind people who carried our family through the horrible ordeal of Alyson's year-long illness and death:

- The wonderful faculty members at Freed-Hardeman University who did my student-teacher observations and took over classes for Ron and me during the fall of 2000. Everyone has lots to do at a Christian college. Everyone has a heavy load, but everyone was willing to shoulder more because of our need.

- People from Freed-Hardeman University, from churches around the country, and kind individuals who generously provided money for all the extra expenses, such as travel and meals connected with having an extremely sick child and grandchild.

- Numerous men who mowed Bryan and Leanne's lawn so they would have more time with Alyson and Meghan.

- The hundreds of people who brought home-cooked meals to the hospital or to Leanne and Bryan's home. We were even brought a full Thanksgiving dinner not long after Alyson's diagnosis. I once said to Vann and Beth, some of the special friends: "I think you should put all of us on your income tax form as a deduction since you have fed us so much during the past few months."

- The special four couples who were at the hospital day and night to take care of physical, emotional, and spiritual needs—Kimberly and Dave, Lisa and Dave, Suzanne and John, Beth and Vann. No friends could have given more than these eight did during the thirteen months of Alyson's illness. Some of them were always at the hospital. They all had jobs, and three of the couples had children of their own. They all had many valid reasons for not helping. They could have easily justified giving minimal help, but they let nothing stand in their way. They saw a need. They were servants who loved God and their fellow brothers and sisters in Christ.

- Kimberly and Dave coordinated all the preparing and transporting of food for Leanne and Bryan on treatment days and every day Alyson was in the hospital. What a tremendous task for thirteen long months! They also served as a clearinghouse for phone calls and emails for Alyson's family. It was such a burden lifted when Bryan and Leanne didn't have to answer the phone or respond to emails. They wanted to hear from everyone, but their energy was consumed with a very sick child and her seven-year-old sibling, Meghan. Kimberly passed on information whenever it was convenient for Bryan and Leanne.

> What a lovely, thoughtful service—one that would have never crossed my mind.

- Jody, the busy minister of a large congregation in Atlanta, bringing us breakfast several mornings during the last few weeks Alyson was in the hospital, always being there to listen, staying the entire night and the morning during Alyson's last hours. He even traveled to Henderson, Tennessee, for a special service for Alyson.

- People who paid for Meghan's school lunches for a year so Leanne would have one less thing to think about. What a lovely, thoughtful service—one that would have never crossed my mind.

- Numerous people who brought or sent gifts to Alyson and Meghan. Many gifts came from other congregations, especially from the Antioch congregation in Nashville. Jill and Kathy, friends of Leanne's brother and sister-in-law, coordinated prayer groups and many cards and gifts for the girls. Although Meghan was not sick, she was never forgotten when presents were sent or brought. Sensitive people remembered that seven is not a large number of years for a little girl.

- Thoughtful people who brought baskets of snacks to the hospital for all of us—fruit, nuts, crackers, cookies, candy, dried fruit, prepared puddings, hot chocolate mix.

- Those who even thought to bring rolls of quarters so we would have change for the cold drink machine.

- For the prayers and kindnesses from friends and relatives, and from those we hardly knew.

- My sweet daughter-in-law, Gina, who paid to have Leanne's house cleaned during the months of treatment.

- Erin, who did the house cleaning at a discount rate to help Leanne and Bryan.

- My mother-in-law, Iola, who kept things together at home when I had to be away so much, especially helping to care for my mother who had dementia.

- My cousin, Martha, who lives in Atlanta, spent many special hours with Meghan during Alyson's illness.

- Brian and Kay, our wonderful son and daughter-in-law, who took me to Atlanta after we learned of Alyson's first relapse. Ron was unable to go. They knew my emotional state would not permit me to drive there safely alone. They also helped care for my mother during my absence.

- Lovely Mrs. Jones, Meghan's former teacher, who visited the hospital often, not only to see Alyson, but especially to take Meghan to lunch. During the summer she even brought some of Meghan's little girlfriends to play in the hospital garden. It was a special treat for Meghan to be the "tour guide" around the hospital. Mrs. Jones thought of so many special things to do for Meghan. After working all day as a teacher, she endured Atlanta traffic to bring Meghan to the hospital from school during the last two months when Alyson was hospitalized. After Alyson died Mrs. Jones supervised all the children who came to the funeral home with their parents so the adults—aunts, uncles, and others— could comfort Bryan and Leanne and themselves without being distracted. On what would have been Alyson's fourth birthday, Mrs. Jones didn't forget Meghan. She took her to buy a book for the preschool library, a book donated in Alyson's name, a children's book Meghan thought a four-year-old would enjoy. I have often made the statement that "everyone should have a Mrs. Jones in her life."

- Those kind people who brought their dogs to visit the hospital. How Alyson loved them. She knew each one by name. "Tiger Lily" was her favorite; she was a gentle pup who often wore a tutu and danced to entertain the children. I know it was a chore for the dog owners, but how

> I know it was a chore for the dog owners, but how delightful for Alyson and the other young cancer patients.

79

delightful the visits were for Alyson and the other young cancer patients.

- Mr. Tone, the clown who visited the hospital. Gently talking to Alyson, he made animals from balloons according to her specifications—blue dogs, yellow cats. Alyson also loved the magic tricks which he did in his quiet, soft-spoken manner.

- Judy, the kind nurse who gave Alyson blood platelets during those last few hours of life when her nose started to bleed, a sign that her little organs were deteriorating. It was as if Judy was breaking the alabaster jar for all of us who were witnessing this terrible scene. Jesus said it was all right for Mary to anoint Him with the expensive perfume as He was being prepared for His death, even though one of His disciples thought it was a waste. Judas questioned why the money had not been given to the poor instead. The blood platelets were not going to heal Alyson. Shouldn't this precious bottle have been used for other sick children who still had the potential for getting well? Judy was willing to do this great thing for Alyson's parents and grandparents to help in a small way to ease the pain of those last terrible hours.

It was as if Judy was breaking the alabaster jar for all of us who were witnessing this terrible scene.

- And for many other caring members of the church—the church, the manifold wisdom of God (Ephesians 3:10). "God sets the solitary in families" (Psalm 68:6 NKJV). "How blessed are those whose strength is in You" (Psalm 84:5 NKJV). In His wisdom, God did not intend for us to be orphans; He gave us a loving family, the church.

With thanksgiving let your
requests be made known to God
and the peace of God, which surpasses
all comprehension, will guard
your hearts and your minds
in Christ Jesus.

Philippians 4:6–7

---

*Alyson, Meghan, and Mom having fun
in Nana and Pop Pop's backyard, October, 1999*

Chapter 11

Thankfulness:
The Antidote to
Bitterness

Gratitude Is Healing

When my children were young I taught them the Scripture: "Rejoice always, pray without ceasing; in everything give thanks" (1 Thessalonians 5:16–18). I especially emphasized that we are to give thanks for everything, both good and bad. I have thought about this Scripture often since Alyson's death. How can I give thanks for the loss of this precious baby? How can I, in any way, be thankful?

Since I taught this Scripture to my children, I decided I needed to learn it myself—not memorize it, but learn it. I began thinking about all the wonderful things that surrounded Alyson during her life and death, and how I could be thankful for them. I must as the psalmist says, "Enter His gates with thanksgiving, and His courts with praise. Give thanks to Him; bless His name. For the Lord is good; His lovingkindness is everlasting" (Psalm 100:4–5).

- *I am thankful that God is protecting us during this time of trial.* "If I take the wings of the dawn, if I dwell in the remotest part of the sea, even there Thy hand will lead me, and Thy right hand will lay hold of me" (Psalm 139:9–10). I love that promise.

- *I am thankful that Leanne and Bryan's marriage is strong enough to weather this powerful storm.* I have been told that ninety percent of marriages break up after the death of a child. I am thankful these two children of mine—my in-law children are as precious as my birth children—find solace in each other in this darkest of times.

- *I am thankful Alyson had a mother and father who loved God and who loved her very much.*

- *I am thankful Alyson had a sister who loved her at all times,* even when Alyson felt sick and yelled at her because she needed to vent her frustrations at someone.

- *I am thankful Alyson had such wonderful care from her parents and sister, from the nurses and doctors at Egleston Hospital, and from caring friends.*

- *I am thankful for modern pain medications,* because leukemia would be much more horrific without them.

- *I am thankful Alyson did not go to Minnesota for the bone marrow transplant if she was not going to make it through the procedure. It was better that she spent her last few days in a place she knew, among familiar nurses, doctors, and friends.*

> It was better that she spent her last few days in a place she knew, among familiar nurses, doctors, and friends.

- *I am thankful that I had wonderful friends who took over many of my college jobs so I could be with Alyson during the last two months of her life.*

- *I am thankful that God gave Leanne, Bryan, and me the strength to endure the many sleepless nights in the hospital without our getting sick.*

- *I am thankful that Caren and Bill, Meghan and Alyson's wonderful grandparents, willingly came to stay many weeks during that year of illness* so they could spend time with both Meghan and Alyson, as we were doing.

- *I am thankful for the absolutely special family summer of 1999 before Alyson was diagnosed with lymphoma in November.* Alyson, her sister, and her mother spent a week with us in Henderson. We also spent a week with all the family in a sun-filled vacation in Florida. That time together was pure joy. I remember reluctantly telling my friend, Jeanine, about the grand summer we were having. Why? Because Jeanine was going through chemotherapy.

- *I am thankful for wonderfully big wagons at the hospital that Alyson could ride around on the third floor of Egleston Hospital when she didn't feel well enough to walk.* What a blessing they were! One night she even slept in one because she loved the cozy comfort of being in a small space when she didn't feel well. I am thankful for the lovely nurse on the night shift who was willing to bend over to take her vital signs so Alyson could continue to stay curled up in the wagon like a sleepy kitten.

- *I am thankful that Bryan and Leanne are trying to give to those who are suffering, things they were given—hope and physical blessings.*

- *I am thankful for God's unfailing love. "The Lord sustains all who fall, and raises up all who are bowed down" (Psalm 145:14). Another precious promise.*

- I am thankful that we got to go to Disney World as a family to spend a few happy days with Alyson before she got too weak to enjoy life. We all needed those happy memories of seeing Alyson's wish fulfilled.

- *I am thankful that God is constantly aware of us and makes us stronger when we feel so weak and vulnerable.* "When He acts on the left, I cannot behold Him; He turns on the right, I cannot see Him. But He knows the way I take; when He has tried me, I shall come forth as gold" (Job 23:9-10).

- *I am thankful that we know that Alyson has a wonderful everlasting life.* "For indeed while we are in this tent, we groan, being burdened, because we do not want to be unclothed, but to be clothed, in order that what is mortal may be swallowed up by life" (2 Corinthians 5:4). Do we really hear what Paul is saying? He isn't saying that what is mortal is swallowed up by death, but by life. That's what heaven is: life in its most perfect form—life that swallows up the mortality of the faithful and gives them the glory of immortality! I am thankful that death is not the end of life, but only the beautiful beginning.

• *I am thankful for God's promise of peace.* There were times during this unthinkable ordeal that a feeling of absolute peace would overtake me. The night and morning when it was obvious that Alyson was dying was one of those times. I felt totally peaceful, totally calm. I was able to comfort others without the need to be comforted. I was able to think rationally and make decisions. I was not overcome with emotion. Tears did not come. I knew this ability was not within my human power. I felt the Lord was answering in me the prayer of Isaiah: "O Lord, be gracious to us; we have waited for Thee. Be Thou their strength every morning, our salvation also in the time of distress" (Isaiah 33:2).

As God promised Isaiah, He also promised me. Isaiah 26:3 says, "The steadfast of mind Thou wilt keep in perfect peace, because he trusts in Thee."

"O Lord, be gracious to us; we have waited for Thee. Be Thou their strength every morning, our salvation also in the time of distress."

As if His hand were actually touching me, I felt God's great comfort. "As one whom his mother comforts, so I will comfort you" (Isaiah 66:13). "Do not fear, for I am with you; do not anxiously look about you, for I am your God. I will strengthen you, surely I will help you, Surely I will uphold you with My righteous right hand" (Isaiah 41:10). "In quietness and trust is your strength" (Isaiah 30:15).

I had felt a terrible storm. I had been besieged by a wicked foe—cancer—but God's righteousness had clothed me with peace so that I could stand firm. "When the whirlwind passes, the wicked is no more, but the righteous has an everlasting foundation" (Proverbs 10:25). I felt His love during those long hours. It gave me a quiet peace. "He will be quiet in His love" (Zephaniah 3:17).

> I had been besieged by a wicked foe—cancer—but God's righteousness had clothed me with peace so that I could stand firm.

By realizing that God was right there grieving with us, I could feel strong. I could feel a joy even in sorrow, a joy of knowing that He would never leave me, that Alyson was now safely tucked under His arm. "The joy of the Lord is your strength" (Nehemiah 8:10).

- *I am thankful for the memory book.* Kimberly put together a lovely book of memories of Alyson and gave it to Bryan, Leanne, and Meghan on what would have been Aly's fourth birthday. The following are excerpts:

    Aly: Look, Kim-buh-ly, look! (pointing to her head) See my hay-uh (hair).
    Kimberly: Oh, yes, I see. It's growing back in. It looks nice; you look nice with or without hair. Aly, you know it may fall out again, but it will grow back.
    Aly: Yeah, I know. It'll grow back. It's not like Dave's. (Dave was balding.)

Matthew and Andrew are Kimberly's and Dave's seven- and four-year-old sons. The following conversation took place one day on the way from the hospital;

> Matthew: I'm sad, Meghan. Are you sad?
>
> Meghan (with a lump in her throat): Yes.
>
> Matthew: Me and Andrew could be your brothers.
>
> Dave: Yes, actually did you know Christians get to call each other brother and sister?
>
> Kimberly: So really, in God's eyes, you really can be part of the same family. (Meghan and Matthew smile, look at each other and giggle.)

Members of the Campus congregation provided the following notes for the memory book:

> "Alyson was a little light that will always shine bright in our lives. Our child prayed that "God would fix Alyson's cells so the two of them could play together again."

> "When I get to heaven, Alyson will be one of the first ones I'll want to see when I get there."

> "When Alyson and my daughter were two years old, they were in the same Sunday school class. My daughter was having a particularly sad day. Alyson, who had already been out of class for some time due to her illness, noticed my daughter's mood. She came right over and got Miranda interested in a game. After succeeding in getting Miranda distracted, Alyson looked over at me and whispered, 'You can go now, she'll be all right. I'll take care of her.' It was so amazing to me that as young as she was and as bad as she was feeling, she could still focus on the needs of others. She was so amazing."

"We had invited several people over to our house for a brunch one Sunday after church and Alyson's family was included. We all had a wonderful time. A few weeks later I was talking to Alyson. I brought up the brunch at our house, Jokingly I told her it would be her turn to cook, because it is hard to cook for that many people. She looked at her mom with a grin and said, 'Okay, I'll just order pizza.' Then she laughed her precious little laugh.

She then drove us all over town from her pretend driver's seat behind the recliner.

"When Alyson was sick I went to see her in the hospital several times. One visit I will never forget. As I came into the room, I saw Leanne, Meghan, and Alyson—all in the same hospital bed laughing hysterically. It was one of the most joyful pictures I have ever seen. After a few minutes Alyson bumped her head and began to cry. She reached for Meghan who hugged her close and hard for probably an entire minute. A peaceful quietness came over Alyson. I will always remember the unity of those three as they laughed together and the tender hug of comfort between two sisters."

"I will never forget Alyson's energy and imagination. One afternoon when I delivered a meal, I found Alyson and Meghan falling all over each other laughing and talking non-stop about how the three of them (including their mother) had been chasing the gerbil around the house after his latest escape. Alyson loved telling me how 'Mommy said she was about to have to get the vacuum and suck him out from behind the couch!' Alyson then promptly told me where to sit and that we were going to pretend that I was the baby. Meghan was to be the cat and she was to be the mom. She then drove us all over town from her pretend driver's seat behind the recliner. Her imagination about where we were headed and what we were seeing on the trip was endless. I left there that day with a smile on my face and joy in my heart because of a very special three-year-old."

Speaking of her first encounter with Alyson, a nineteen-year-old said, "I noticed how she smiled at everyone who passed by and how she had a laugh that could brighten anyone's gloomiest day." Excerpts from her memories also included the following:

"I was given the opportunity to work at the Emory Clinic during the summer, which was only a block from where Aly spent her days in the hospital. My visits to see her were always the highlight of my busy workdays. I believe the main reason God led me to that job was so I could be close to Aly. She is someone I came to know as a sister and a friend. She taught me more than any other human being that I know. As a child she has shown me that no matter how old you are or how helpless your life, nothing can keep you from smiling. She bestowed upon me the greatest of honors when she called me her 'biggest best girl friend.' That is something that will always be a part of me."

(This young woman has since decided to become a teacher, partly because of Alyson's influence.)

• *I am thankful that Leanne and Bryan have wonderful friends.* One friend, John, wrote the following beautiful and mean-ingful song and sang it for Alyson's funeral celebration:

Play with the Angels
(Alyson's Song)

Open Your arms, Lord;
Receive our little one.
Take her and hold her
For we no longer can.
She'll make You happy.
Oh, what a precious child.
She's reaching out to You;
Please come and take her hand.
Take her to play with the angels,
Where she'll be free to laugh and run.
Now, though it feels we are losing,
Living with You means she has won.
Our hearts are breaking.
We cannot understand.
What is the reason
That she couldn't stay?
But You will be with us
With Your love and comfort,
Holding our hand
Every step of the way.
Now she can play with the angels.
Now she is free to laugh and run.
Now, though it feels we have lost her,
Living with You means she has won.

Even for this tragedy, I am told to give thanks "in every-thing" (1 Thessalonians 5:18). I am not to be anxious about anything, "but in everything by prayer and supplication *with thanksgiving*," to present my request to God. Even during the greatest distress, I am told to give thanks. And then comes the great promise: "And the peace of God, which surpasses all comprehension, shall guard your hearts and your minds in Christ Jesus" (Philippians 4:6–7). God has granted me this wonderful peace—a peace that comes through thanksgiving.

God often gives joy along with sorrow. On November 23, 2001, a year and one week after Alyson's death, Andrew Reid joined Bryan, Leanne, and Meghan's family. He has a sister, Alyson, who lives in heaven. He will learn about her as he grows. He will learn that she helped name him. She always played "Dr. Reid." Neither I nor any of my family believe Andrew was in any way sent to take Alyson's place. Neither was he sent to be overshadowed by a "ghost child" who can do no wrong. He is a precious little blessing in his own right. Leanne believes his sunny little personality is a true gift from God provided during their time of grieving.

> Leanne believes his sunny little personality is a true gift from God provided during their time of grieving.

When Andrew came home from the hospital to live in his home with his parents and his wonderful big sister, Meghan, his father, Bryan, petitioned God in a prayer I will never forget: "Dear God. Thank you for this sweet baby boy. Please let us keep him for a long time and help him to grow up to be a fine Christian man."

I am thankful this book doesn't end with death. It begins with death: it ends with life and hope.

A New Battle

On January 17, 2007, just as the final arrangements for printing this book were being made, I received an implausible call from my son, Keith, who lives in Nashville. Among sobs he said, "Mom, we have bad news. Matthew has a malignant tumor in his bladder." Time stood still as I tried to comprehend the words. My two-and-one-half-year-old grandson, the youngest of four brothers, has cancer. How can this possibly be true? How can all of us face this again?

Later that day as I stood with friends from several Nashville congregations in a lobby of the children's hospital at Vanderbilt, I heard elders and other Christian men pray for our baby, his parents, and his brothers, David, Stephen, and Jonathan. I shivered as I remembered hearing the same heartfelt prayers in Egleston Hospital seven years ago.

After the prayer, one person said, "This must be extremely hard for you because of your other grandchild." I answered,

"It is, but God doesn't say life won't be difficult. He only asks us to be faithful during these bad times."

I don't know the outcome of this yet-another battle in our lives. My daughter, Leanne, said she dreamed last night that she saw little Matthew grown up—Dr. Matthew Butterfield—and lecturing to medical students about childhood cancer. If only dreams could come true.

We are constantly praying for Matthew's complete healing. My family and I beg you to pray for him also, as well as for this brothers and for his dad and mom, Keith and Gina Butterfield.

> Pray one for another that ye may
> be healed. The effectual fervent prayer
> of a righteous man availeth much.

James 5:16 KJV

In His love,

Edna Butterfield

Works Cited

Bush, Barbara. *Barbara Bush: A Memoir*, New York: St. Martin's Paperbacks, 1995.

Lawrence, Don H. "Sunrise," columns in *Chester County Independent Newspaper*, Henderson, TN.

Morrell, David. *Desperate Measures*, New York: Warner Books, Inc., 1994.

Richman, Linda. *I'd Rather Laugh*, New York: Warner Books, Inc., 2001.

Schwiebert, Pat, Deklyen, Chuck, & Bills, Taylor. *Tear Soup*, Portland, OR: Grief Watch, 1999.

Sittser, Gary. *A Grace Disguised*, Grand Rapids, MI: Zondervan Publishing House, 1995.